TACKLE RUGBY

TACKLE RUGBY

Bill Beaumont

with Ian Robertson

Stanley Paul

London Sydney Auckland Melbourne Johannesburg

Stanley Paul & Co. Ltd

An imprint of the Hutchinson Publishing Group

17–21 Conway Street, London W1P 6JD

Hutchinson Group (Australia) Pty Ltd
30–32 Cremorne Street, Richmond South, Victoria 3121
PO Box 151, Broadway, New South Wales 2007

Hutchinson Group (N Z) Ltd
32–34 View Road, PO Box 40–086, Glenfield, Auckland 10

Hutchinson Group (S A) Pty Ltd
PO Box 337, Bergvlei 2012, South Africa

First published 1983
© Bill Beaumont 1983

Set in Univers Light

Printed in Great Britain by The Anchor Press Ltd
and bound by Wm Brendon & Son Ltd,
both of Tiptree, Essex

British Library Cataloguing in Publication Data

ISBN 0 09 153600 6 (cased)
      0 09 153601 4 (paper)

Frontispiece: *Huw Davies about to side-step past
Roger Baird in the 1983 Calcutta Cup match at
Twickenham*

Contents

Acknowledgements

I should like to thank Ian Robertson for all his help in the preparation of this book and also the boys from Stoneyhurst School in Lancashire who braved the elements on a series of bitterly cold afternoons to demonstrate so expertly the skills of rugby. I should like to thank in particular their games master, Dick Greenwood, for all his help and cooperation, and the redoubtable Mike Brett, whose exceptional talents as a photographer will be appreciated by all who study the pictures in this book. Finally, I am indebted to the posse of typists headed by Jackie Valledy who rushed frantically to meet the deadline.

A determined burst by Paul Dodge for England against Australia at Twickenham in 1982

Introduction

Rugby is really a very simple game, and if every player took the trouble to master all the basic skills, then both the individual and the team would derive far more pleasure, satisfaction and enjoyment from the game. No matter how complex a particular manoeuvre may look during a match, everything is completely dependent on a good sound grounding in the essential techniques of the game.

As a youngster I played fullback and fly half for ten years and I learned to pass, kick and tackle as well as any threequarter. This stood me in good stead throughout my career. Every player should be competent in these simple techniques. Any forward at any time in a match may find himself part of a two-against-one overlap, and he must be able to give and take a pass, draw an opponent and time the whole manoeuvre with precision or he will let down his team-mates. Similarly, any self-respecting back must know exactly what to do in a ruck or a maul to help his forwards secure possession.

There is a natural tendency for players to practise what they are good at and ignore those aspects of the game which they either do badly or do not enjoy. This means many players nowadays, even at the highest level, only kick well with one foot or tackle well with one shoulder or pass well in only one direction. Too many players even reach international level with obvious deficiencies, and they can spend a great deal of time trying to cover up their shortcomings. It is so much easier to put in the necessary hours of practice as a schoolboy, with the guarantee that, like riding a bicycle, once the correct technique has been acquired it will never be forgotten. All the important team skills rely on a mastery of the individual skills.

In this book, the boys of Stoneyhurst School demonstrate, with the help of easy-to-follow illustrations, the whole range of the basic skills required for both backs and forwards. My aim is to show, as simply as possible, how to pass, catch, break, tackle, kick, scrummage, ruck, maul, and win line-out ball. The same straightforward technique will be successful at whatever standard the game is played, from mini-rugby to international level, but the sooner the individual player gets to grips with it, the better he will be.

By following the clear illustrations and the concise text in this book, I hope it will be easy for everyone to acquire the various skills. I have stressed in each chapter the need to progress carefully in stages. It is important to build gradually on a sound technique rather than try to assimilate too much too quickly.

In coaching youngsters, I have devised a series of simple practice routines which can be used in any training session to develop particular skills. At the end of each section in the book, I have included those that I found to be the most effective. They are invariably carried out in pairs or small groups, and should be of great benefit to both individual players and the whole team.

Patience will prove to be a great virtue, but always remember that rugby should be fun. Training, practising and playing should be equally enjoyable, but it ought to go without saying that the higher the standard you reach, and the fewer mistakes made by you and your team, the greater the satisfaction and pleasure you will get from the game.

I hope this book explains everything in such clear, straightforward terms that rugby will be restored to the simple game it really is, so enabling the next generation to enjoy all the fun, excitement and thrills which I experienced in twenty exceptionally happy years in the game. All the hours of dedicated practice will prove worthwhile in the end.

1 Passing and Catching

PASSING

At its best rugby is a running, handling game, and no matter the strengths of a team at any given time, it is essential that every player is competent in catching and passing the ball.

It has struck me over the years that at training sessions youngsters spend far too much time practising kicking the ball and far too little time running up and down the pitch perfecting their handling. Part of the reason for this may lie in the fact that it is easier and more fun to practise drop goals and place kicks than to cover thirty lengths of the pitch practising handling at the start of each session. But it should be remembered that the success of any side is more likely to depend on the ability of fifteen players to give and take a pass rather than on the place-kicking skills of all fifteen.

From the beginning, it is important to master this vital art. Even now, at international level, it is easy to find backs who are not good passers, and this can be traced to a lack of discipline and practise at an early age. It is hard to correct the errors of a lifetime; it is much easier to make sure you get it right from the start.

Passing is not one of the easiest skills to master. If I was able to catch and pass a shade better than most other 16-stone locks it was probably because I had the distinct advantage of having played at fullback and fly half for eight years at school. To pass well requires a combination of several different skills at the same time: balance, accuracy, agility and timing. It is also important to be able to pass equally well to either side.

Paul Dodge, England and Lions centre, committing Fergus Slattery during an England-Ireland international whilst carefully lining up his pass to Clive Woodward on his right

The basic process is illustrated here in three simple movements.

1. The player holding the ball in front of him with both hands turns his head towards the receiver and prepares to propel the ball in front of the receiver to ensure that he runs onto it with both hands outstretched. If the player passes directly at the receiver's stomach, this forces the receiver to check his stride and slows the whole movement down. This is the first golden rule: pass in front of the receiver and not at him, or, worst of all, behind him.

2. The pass should be delivered in a simple, flowing action with your eyes fixed just in front of the receiver. Your hands guide the ball accurately as they sweep across the front of your body, and at the moment of delivery your weight is predominantly on your right leg when, as in this illustration, you pass to your left.

3. The moment the ball leaves your hands travelling to your left, your body will naturally fall away in the opposite direction, with your left leg crossing over in front of your right leg. The body movement demonstrated here gives the pass accuracy and power, and has the advantage of committing your immediate opponent to following you. This, in effect, takes him temporarily out of the game, because if he begins to drift towards the receiver before you release the ball, you will be able to beat him by selling a dummy.

The pass to the right is executed in exactly the same manner. Your weight at the moment of delivery is on your left leg and your body falls naturally away to your left as your right leg crosses over in front. Once your weight is transferred onto your right leg, the very next step with your left leg should be a drag to your right to support the ball.

England fly half Huw Davies passing left for Cambridge University against Steele-Bodgers XV – a model of concentration, commitment and accuracy

PRACTICE

The simplest way to practise passing until it becomes second nature is to begin moving along the touch line at walking pace and, without even using a ball at first, go through the motions of passing. By starting a few inches on the right side of the line and practising passing to your left, you will quickly find that your left leg will cross the line as you fall away after executing the pass. By passing to your right the reverse will happen. Once you have mastered this at walking pace, you can gradually build up speed until you are able to do it flat out.

At this juncture a ball can be introduced and, once passing becomes instinctive, you can practise by running at a goal post, falling away on either side of the post until you can do it automatically.

Nowadays there are variations on this theme: in New Zealand and South Africa they tend to pass in a less exaggerated manner. But before learning the variations, it is vital to master the basics and an intuitive knowledge of this type of pass will always stand you in good stead. Once the skill has been perfected, you can try to increase the speed of transfer without losing any accuracy.

1. One method of practising quick passing is to work up and down the field in groups of three, with each person taking turns to be in the middle.

2. It is worth noting in this illustration that, as the first person releases the ball, the receiver in the middle already has both hands outstretched to catch it as early as possible in its flight.

3. The outstretched hands are an excellent target to encourage the passer to guide the ball in front of the receiver. Always remember that, like when trying to catch a cricket ball thrown directly at you, you should not hug the ball into your chest but take it in front of you in both hands. This saves the valuable time you would otherwise need to readjust the ball before passing it on.

4. The split second you are in complete control, turn your head and body towards the third player in the group and whip the ball in front of him as quickly and as accurately as possible.

5. At the same time, fall away after the pass to check and commit any would-be opponent.

This drill improves the middle player's speed and accuracy of passing to each side. It is remarkable how much improvement can be achieved with regular practice.

SUMMARY

1. Good balance is important. Make sure you pass off the correct leg and fall away after delivering the pass, rather than running towards the receiver.
2. Always look where you are passsing. Your head should be turned as far round as possible and your eyes should be fixed on a point in front of the receiver.
3. Develop a good rhythm. Your arms should sweep across in front of the body at about waist height in a single smooth movement.
4. A good follow-through with the hands ensures accuracy and a good trajectory. After the pass, your hands should finish up pointing, and your eyes staring, at the target area – with luck, the outstretched hands of the receiver.

5. The body should remain more or less upright throughout the manoeuvre.
6. Keep practising until you can pass equally well to either side. Always try to improve your speed and accuracy. Length of pass is not as important as speed and accuracy.
7. The moment you have completed the pass and fallen away, with your next step forward you should drive off in the direction of your pass to support the ball.

Once you have mastered the art of orthodox passing, every other aspect of handling, including the whole range of manoeuvres to beat a man, will fall into place. It will prove well worth the endless hours of practice, but, remember, it is just about the hardest skill to acquire and it does demand great patience and perseverance.

CATCHING

As we have seen, the best way of catching the ball in a normal passing movement is to take it in both hands in front of the body, ready for a quick transfer. The technique for catching a high kick is quite different, although several of the basic essentials remain the same.

1. As we see here, balance is important. Your head should be tilted upwards to allow your eyes to be fixed on the ball for the whole time it is in the air. If you take your eyes off the ball, even for a split second, you will break your concentration and find it desperately difficult to pick up the precise flight path of the ball when you try to focus on it again. Ideally, you should spring to the spot where you can expect the ball to land and, if possible, be stationary when you actually make the catch. It is much easier to take the ball standing still than it is to catch it on the move.

2. The catcher in this sequence has successfully got under the ball and is ready to make the catch.

3. He has a firm, solid base, with feet about a shoulder-width apart, and he has cradled his arms with fingers pointing skywards ready to clutch the ball into his chest. Elbows, like feet, should be about a shoulder-width apart to prevent the ball from slipping straight through.

4. Simultaneously, as your hands and arms engulf the ball and hug it firmly to your chest, your body should turn side on to the opposition and your knees should bend a little on impact.

The reasons for turning side on are twofold.

First, if the opposition happen to arrive at the same time as the ball, you will then present them with a solid and well-protected target. With your elbows tucked in, there are no vulnerable areas and the risk of injury is minimized. Secondly, should the ball be dropped, it is not a knock-on if it spills sideways and the player then has a chance to recover and tidy up.

PRACTICE

The best way to practise is in pairs, with each player throwing the ball in the air to his partner. Once a good success rate is achieved with the players standing only a few metres apart, the distance and height the ball is thrown in the air can be extended. As confidence is developed, the players can stand about 15 metres apart and lob kicks at each other. The height of the kicks should be increased gradually and, when the players are confident under the high ball, they can experience the extra pressure of a match situation created by a couple of attackers running at them in pursuit of the kick-ahead.

SUMMARY

1. Keep your eyes fixed on the ball all the time. Ignore the opposition.
2. Form a basket for the ball with your hands, arms, elbows and chest.
3. Have a solid base, with your feet a shoulder-width apart.
4. Be side on to the opposition as you catch the ball.

2 Scrum-Half Passing

If I look back on my rugby career and single out the one position where I was relieved to have a really good player in my team, scrum half probably tops the list. The scrum half's most important asset is his pass, which should be fast, accurate and of reasonable length. Over and above this, it is a bonus if he acts as an extra flank forward in defence and rips the opposition defence asunder with explosive bursts from the set piece or the loose. No one will complain if his line kicking is long and accurate as well, but the first priority must be his pass.

There are four basic types of scrum-half pass and not only should the scrum half be thoroughly competent in all four, but he should also be able to pass with the same facility off either hand. Too many scrum halfs concentrate on superb, long spin-passing off their stronger hand and ignore the other hand altogether. From the very start, a keen scrum half should practise passing equally to right and left. The technique is exactly the same for either side, but, remember, to reach a high standard requires months, if not years, of practice.

In this chapter we illustrate the four basic passes: from the ground after a scrum or run; from waist height after a line-out or maul; the dive pass; and the reverse pass.

Nigel Melville demonstrating the perfect position to deliver a pass from a line-out during England's match against Western America

ORTHODOX PASS FROM THE GROUND

In this sequence the scrum half demonstrates the technique for passing to the left. It is important to get the feet in the right position so that the pass can be executed in one continuous flowing movement.

1. As the ball is about to surface from the scrum or ruck, the scrum half should be crouching forward, hands open near the ground, with the foot farther away from the receiver beside the ball. In this case, the ball will be beside the toe of his right boot with the player's head directly over the ball, his eyes fixed on it and his bodyweight mainly on the right leg.

2. The hands grasp the ball ready to pass, with the right hand on top and at the side to give a powerful pass, while the left hand is underneath on the other side to control the direction and ensure accuracy. Your body should be as low as possible and, as you are about to pass, your head should begin to turn towards the receiver and you should begin to transfer your weight from your right leg to your left.

3. By the time you are releasing the ball, your weight should be on your left leg and your eyes fixed on the target area in front of the receiver.

4. As your body uncoils, your hands should follow right through while your hips, head and shoulders rotate towards the receiver.

ORTHODOX PASS FROM LINE-OUT OR MAUL

In exactly the same way as with the pass from the ground, to ensure speed of delivery the crucial factors are the positioning of the feet, hands and body. The split second the ball emerges from the line-out or maul, the scrum half must get into position so that he can fire out his pass in one continuous action.

1. When passing to the left, to prevent any delay he should aim to take the ball just to his right-hand side with his hands extended, his eyes riveted on the ball and his weight primarily on his right leg.

2. Taking the ball as early as possible and lowering the body a little on maximum momentum, the weight is transferred towards the left leg. At the same time, the body swings round to the left, dropping lower, with the head turning and the eyes fixed on the target area in front of the receiver.

3. The head should be brought up on the follow-through and, as the body uncoils, the weight should now be primarily on the left leg. The hands must follow right through across the body, with the power coming from the right hand in this instance and the guiding accuracy from the left. When passing to the right, the reverse is the case – the power will come from the left hand and the guiding accuracy from the right.

THE DIVE PASS

There are occasions when the orthodox pass from the ground presents special difficulties, such as when your pack are beating a retreat at a scrum, or producing poor-quality, badly channelled ball, or inaccurate, wild palming from the line-out. Inevitably such manoeuvres greatly increase the pressure on the scrum half and, with half the opposition poised to attack him, it is not practical to send out a normal orthodox pass. In such circumstances, the scrum half is best advised to dive pass. Under pressure, this gives him more control and can be executed more quickly than trying to scamper into position for an orthodox pass. It is particularly useful in coping with a wet ball on a heavy pitch. The first essential is to pass off one foot rather than off both feet. It does not make any difference which foot he passes off; it depends which leg happens to arrive beside the ball first. But, remember, a great deal of momentum and drive will be lost if the pass is attempted off both feet.

1. One foot lands beside the ball with the other foot well behind. In this illustration, the scrum half is about to place his left foot by the ball; it is this leg which provides the main thrust and power as he passes.

2. As the scrum half picks up the ball, with his weight on his left leg, he should at the same time turn his head towards the receiver, with his eyes fixed on the target area in front of the receiver. As he unwinds, his hands lead his body as they drive the ball through a sweeping arc. His head should be kept well up as his whole bodyweight is propelled forward and upward.

3. The scrum half should land a few feet from the takeoff point, head and hands pointing at the receiver. He should then spring quickly back onto his feet and follow the ball in support.

THE REVERSE PASS

In the same set of circumstances which encourage a dive pass, the reverse pass can be a potent weapon if the ball arrives unexpectedly and the scrum half finds he has no time to adjust the positioning of his feet. This is the hardest pass to do well, but it can be devastatingly effective. Just like all the other types of pass, it relies on good feet positioning, balance, quick hands and quick reactions.

1. Scrum half should first have taken a quick glance over his right shoulder to see the position of his fly half. As with all scrum-half passes, the weight is mainly on one leg at the start of the pass, with the head directly over the ball and the eyes fixed on it. The feet should be a shoulder-width apart to give a solid, wide stance and, as he is about to unleash his pass, the scrum half should take a second quick glance at the receiver to gauge exactly where to pass.

2. At the moment the pass is delivered, the bodyweight is transferred to the right leg as the ball is propelled away. The impetus comes from the hands, arms and shoulders working in harmony. In this case, the power comes from the right hand and the guiding control from the left.

3. Both hands follow through in the direction of the receiver.

This is an extremely difficult pass to do well and requires countless hours of practice, but if it is eventually mastered, it can look stunningly spectacular.

23

PRACTICE

The scrum half should stand in midfield with a player in front of him to feed him the ball. A few yards behind him, a couple of fly halfs should be in position, one to his right-hand side and the other to his left. The player feeding the ball to the scrum half kicks, bounces or throws it towards him and simultaneously shouts left or right. As quickly as possible, the scrum half gets to the ball and, depending on the quality of possession, chooses one of the four basic passes to feed the designated fly half. When passing to his weaker side, he should not be encouraged to 'pirouette' pass by turning right round to use his stronger hand. After months of practice, he should develop all four types of pass and acquire an equal facility off either hand.

SUMMARY

1. Speed and accuracy are the first essentials of a good scrum half and throughout his career he should work at clipping a split second off the time he takes to deliver a pass, trying to achieve his optimum distance and striving for ever greater accuracy.
2. Good feet positioning for every type of pass is crucial.
3. No matter how good his technique, a scrum half relies on strong hands, arms and shoulders.
4. Remember to make use of the momentum from the legs, body and shoulders in delivering the pass.
5. Always look at the receiver as you unleash the ball and make sure the pass is in front of him.

Clive Woodward in perfect position to draw his man and to deliver an accurate pass

On the attack for England against Scotland in the final leg of the Grand Slam

3 Running in Attack

The key to good back play is the ability to pass well and run straight. If the art of passing has been successfully mastered, then the full range of attacking manoeuvres should follow without too much difficulty. But if these ploys are to work, it is essential that the players are running at the correct angles. For most attacking moves nowadays, those angles should be parallel to the touch line and not diagonally across the field.

Far too many teams allow their backs to drift across the pitch, which means that even if they do manage to carve out the occasional opening, the cover defence are comfortably able to stifle the danger. The ideal situation which the bulk of set moves tries to initiate is one that finishes up with two attackers being left to confront one defender. The most common moves involve the fullback joining the threequarter line, usually outside the outside centre, but, occasionally, either between the centres or even outside the wing. As long as all the threequarters and the fullback are running straight (parallel to the touch line), the overlap should produce the desired results. Cover defence should check on the penultimate attacker, which should leave the player on the extreme flank in the clear.

There are, of course, several moves which are practised by most rugby teams, but I am not a great believer in teams becoming too preoccupied with dozens of set moves to the detriment of individual skills and natural ability. None the less, when an overlap has been created, it is important that players can translate that advantage into tries and this chapter deals with the individual skills required for this rather than the unit skills. The majority of these set moves produces good second-phase possession, and it is from broken play that good players ought to be able to rip defences apart.

In attack, the worst crime is to squander a two-to-one overlap. This is the classic situation which occurs in every match but does not always produce a try.

1. In this sequence, we see the player running with the ball and straightening up the angle of his approach to draw the sole defender towards him.

2. By running straight rather than drifting across the field, and by dipping into the defender as he is about to pass, the attacker has totally committed his opponent.

3. The timing of the delivery of the pass is crucial and here the attacker, having committed the defender, passes a couple of metres before he reaches him to leave his colleague free outside him. The distance at which the pass is made depends on the relative speed of the two players but it should not be necessary to wait until the last moment.

4. It is worth noting here that the ball has been passed accurately in front of the receiver, who has taken it on the burst in both hands without having to check his stride.

If, of course, the attacker feels at any stage before he passes that the defender is going to ignore him and make for the unmarked man on the overlap, then he can threaten even more trouble for the defending side by selling a dummy to leave his team in complete control with a two-to-none overlap.

1. As the attacker approaches his opponent, he can see the defender is inclining towards the unmarked man.

2. At this stage, sensing he has not totally, or even remotely, committed the defender, the attacker can go through all the motions of passing, but, by hanging onto the ball — that is, by selling a dummy — he can break through himself.

3. As he dips inside, he should straighten up at once and be ready to link up on the outside again.

One of the most useful methods to beat a good defence is the sudden switch of direction. This can be achieved by a scissors in which two players run at completely different angles and cross over.

1. The player with the ball should veer off a straight line to commit his opposite number to follow him diagonally across the pitch.

2. The moment he sets off on this diagonal run, his colleagues outside him should accelerate from a slightly deeper position than usual in a hard straight line parallel to the touch line to take the ball on the burst. The first player should always turn his back to the opposition when he is about to deliver the pass so that they cannot see exactly what is happening and also to protect the ball fully. He should give the receiver a gentle lobbed pass, before sprinting off without the ball along his chosen diagonal path, hoping to lure one or two of the defence after him.

3. After the scissors the receiver continues the attack at a completely different angle to that of the initial ball-carrier. This is bound to present certain difficulties for the defence and should catch them off balance. By exploding through parallel to the touch line, the receiver can choose support players on either side to help him continue the attack, or, at worst, win the ruck or maul if he should be tackled.

In the same way, the player with the ball can, if he sees any sign of hesitancy or uncertainty amongst the opposition, execute a dummy scissors and continue the attack himself.

1. To do this he should still veer off a straight line and cut diagonally in front of the intended receiver.

2. Once again, he should turn his back towards the opposition to conceal and protect the ball, hoping to convince them that he intends to pass. The key figure is the man without the ball. The would-be receiver must run so hard and with such determination that he convinces the opposition he is about to take the ball on the burst.

3. This should cause a momentary hesitation in the opposition ranks, which gives the ball-carrier the opportunity to accelerate through on his diagonal run before quickly straightening his angle to look for support on either side.

PRACTICE

These skills are best practised in groups of three with players taking turns to act as the two attackers and one defender. In a restricted area, perhaps between the halfway line and the 10-metre line, the two attackers should run at the defender and see how near they come to a 100 per cent success in beating him. They have the choice to draw the man and pass the ball, sell a dummy, or execute a scissors or a dummy scissors, depending on the approach of the defender. When the players have mastered the two-against-one situation, they can progress to having three attackers against two defenders in a slightly less confined area. These

exercises should be practised by the forwards as well as the backs. Too often I have seen a front five forward fail to make the most of a two-to-one attacking situation. It is something every player ought to be capable of turning to positive advantage. This is the most basic part of an ability to read the game.

Huw Davies sprinting away from John Rutherford (10) and Norman Rowan in the 1981 England– Scotland match

SUMMARY

1. Remember the importance of straight running.

2. The timing of the pass or the selling of the dummy is crucial to its success.

3. Commit your opponent and, if possible, the cover defence before you pass or have a go yourself if the opportunity arises.

4. Always look for support players, but only pass to someone in a better position than you.

5. In any manoeuvre the player acting as a decoy – not receiving the ball – is the most important player on the pitch. He must convince the whole world he is definitely going to receive the ball. It is no use simply going through the motions because you know you are not going to be passed the ball. If you do that, the opposition will not pay much attention to you. This applies to all back moves which involve missing out one player, such as the various 'miss' moves when the fullback enters the line.

6. Any player going for an opening, trying to make a break, should accelerate and explode at the opposition and not slow down or hesitate.

4 Tackling

Tackling is not normally the favourite aspect of the game for most young players but it is vital in rugby. The sooner youngsters learn to tackle well with either shoulder, the more enjoyment they will eventually derive and the better players they will be. The basic ingredients which tackling demands are courage, determination, unwavering concentration, agility, timing and confidence. The best advice I can give to any player who is wary of becoming too involved in tackling is to learn the right technique early on and then practice regularly until he has complete self-confidence.

A good technique minimizes the fear or risk of injury and can help to develop an appetite and relish for what can be one of the most rewarding aspects of the game. Most people prefer scoring tries to putting in a really satisfying tackle, but, as a lock forward myself, with strictly limited opportunities for helping myself to tries, I gleaned great pleasure from slotting in a few crunching tackles during a match.

There are four basic types of tackle and in this chapter we examine each of them: the side-on tackle, the head-on tackle, the tackle from behind and the smother tackle.

Bill Beaumont lining up Elgan Rees as the Lions wing breaks clear during the England–Wales match in England's Grand Slam season in 1980

Beaumont drives off one leg as he prepares to tackle Rees and bring him to ground

SIDE-ON TACKLE

The tackler should line up his opponent at an angle which enables him to drive in with his shoulder and the momentum of his full body-weight as the attacker is about to run past.

1. The tackler should drive into the tackle off one leg, not two, and, ideally, it should be the same leg as the shoulder he is using for that particular tackle. Launching off one leg gives far greater impetus and power to the tackle.

2. The tackler in this sequence drives off his right leg, which means he hits the attacker with his right shoulder halfway between the knees and the hips and with the momentum of his full bodyweight behind him. At the same time, with his head moving safely behind his opponent's legs, he should firmly encircle his opponent with both hands.

3. To ensure halting the player completely, he should firmly wrap his arms right round the attacker's legs until both arms meet.

4. The combination of the speed, momentum and tight grip will not only be sure to bowl the attacker over, but will also more likely than not leave the tackler on top and in a position to play the ball first.

HEAD-ON TACKLE

The same basic principles required for the side-on tackle apply equally well to the head-on tackle.

1. The defender should drive into the tackle off one leg. In this case, the defender is about to drive off his right leg and will hit the attacker with his right shoulder at about waist level.

2. At the moment of impact, the defender's hand should slip safely to one side while he wraps both arms tightly round the attacker's legs.

3. By hanging on tightly with both arms linked together, he will bring the attacker to the ground.

If both defender and attacker are running at about the same speed, the attacker will probably be knocked up in the air and will land at the side of the tackler. If the tackler is moving faster, he will probably knock the attacker up and backwards. However, if the attacker is travelling faster or is a much bigger and heavier player than the defender, then he will fall forward and land on top of the defender.

If a small fly half has to tackle a large prop forward peeling round from a line-out, he would be well advised not to drive flat out into him, but simply stand his ground and, as the heavier player tries to drive straight through him, dip the shoulder into his midriff and wrap both arms tightly round his legs. His opponent's greater momentum will carry him forward, but he will still finish up on the ground.

TACKLE FROM BEHIND

Once again, a similar technique is used to execute the tackle from behind.

1. The tackler drives off one leg for maximum impetus and sinks one shoulder into the attacker halfway between the knees and hips, keeping his head safely outside the attacker's legs.

2. As he makes initial contact, he should wrap his arms quickly round the attacker's legs, gripping him firmly.

3. The combination of the defender's full bodyweight, speed, drive and tightly bound grip will rapidly bring the attacker down.

PRACTICE

Players should learn how to tackle at an early age, but they should be encouraged to progress gradually and not be rushed into something they are unlikely to relish initially.

Find a partner of roughly the same size and start practising the correct technique at walking pace. One player holding a ball walks along the touch line, while his partner, also at walking pace, tackles him side on.

Take it in turns and practise using the right and left shoulders alternately. As confidence develops and players realize that by using the right technique they are unlikely to be hurt, the tempo can be gradually increased.

During regular training sessions, spread over several weeks, the players can practise at trotting speed, half pace, three-quarter speed and, finally, flat out. This should only be attempted when both partners are technically competent and inwardly confident. The other types of tackle should be learned in similar, gradual stages.

SMOTHER TACKLE

The smother tackle is specifically designed to stop the player with the ball passing to any of his colleagues in order to allow the attack to continue for scoring, if he is close to the goal line. This form of tackle has become increasingly popular in recent years, although it does require a slightly different technique.

1. The defender still drives into the tackle off one leg, but instead of going in low, he attempts to smother his opponent's arms and the ball in one all-embracing high tackle.

2. In this instance, he drives off his right leg and hits his opponent mostly with his right shoulder. The tackler tightly wraps his arms right round the attacker's body in a pincer movement, pinning his arms and the ball at the same time. The driving momentum produced by the tackler as he hits the attacker with his shoulder and arm will knock his opponent off balance.

3. By pulling down hard and clinging on firmly with both arms, the tackler will now be able to force his opponent to the ground unable to release the ball because of the smother tackle.

SUMMARY

The coach who pushes a non-swimmer into the deep end of the pool to force him to learn to swim quickly will not necessarily produce an instant water baby or an enthusiastic participant. Similarly in rugby, forcing youngsters to endure hours of crash tackling practice is the last way to develop this skill. The correct technique is essential and must be taught gradually.

1. Always drive into the tackle off one leg.
2. Wrap your arms tightly round the attacker and cling on with determination.
3. Learn to tackle with either shoulder with equal facility.
4. With the exception of the smother tackle, the target area for every tackle will be somewhere between knee and waist height.

5 Kicking

Despite the fact that rugby is meant to be a running, handling game, most players who turn up early for a training session use the extra time at their disposal to practise kicking. When I think of how much time players spend kicking, it is surprising how badly it is usually done during a match.

The explanation is probably quite simple – poor technique. Players who never learned the correct technique at the outset will doubtless spend the rest of their lives practising for hours on end, but find, to their amazement, that they never seem to improve. Unfortunately, no matter how much time is spent kicking, if the basic technique contains one or two faults, the end product will always be unsatisfactory.

If players want to improve, they must learn the right way to hold the ball, make sure they release it at the correct angle onto their boot, ensure the ball and the boot meet properly, and check they have a good follow-through. In this chapter we will examine the three most important types of kick: the punt, using both right and left feet; the drop kick; and the place kick.

England and Lions fullback Dusty Hare showing an exemplary follow-through in the match against America in Hartford, Connecticut

PUNT

The most important thing to remember about punting a rugby ball is that timing and technique are far more useful than brute strength. Once again, the best way to learn is in a series of simple stages and, to begin with, it is sensible not to try to kick the ball too far. Eventually distance will be achieved, but initially it is best simply to concentrate on making certain each part of the kick is done correctly.

1. The ball should be held at a slight angle and fractionally tilted away from the kicker as in the illustration. The right hand is at the near end of the ball, partly on top but spreading round the side as well. The left hand is at the far end of the ball, partly underneath and partly at the side of it.

2. Take one step forward to place the body-weight on the left leg and, at the same time, drop the ball, at exactly the same angle as it was being held at, straight down towards the ground. Do not throw the ball up in the air before kicking it, but always release it, or even push it straight down.

3. As the ball drops, your right foot should swing through to meet it at exactly the same angle and at the same slight inclination at which it was when it left your hands. Bodyweight momentum should be travelling gently forward, which means it is wrong to be leaning back. Your head should be well over the ball and your eyes fixed on it.

If you compare the angle of the ball on impact with the angle in the very first picture in this sequence, you will notice the marked similarity. Releasing, or pushing the ball down, means that it usually stays at precisely the right angle, but throwing it up in the air before kicking inevitably changes its position in mid-air and makes your kick far more difficult.

4. Your right instep held horizontally should meet the ball roughly twelve inches off the ground. Your toe should be pointed; your eyes still fixed on the ball.

5. After impact, a good high follow-through is essential with the right leg straight and the right foot pointed and fully extended. The weight is still on the left leg and at the point of impact the body will lean back slightly.

The punt should be one continuous smooth action, and the key to success is timing. The technique for the left-footed punt is exactly the same as for the right and the sooner you begin to practise with your left foot, the more likely you are to persevere and make a decent fist of it. Far too many players, even at the highest level of the game, are predominantly one-footed and that is inexcusable. Every back ought to be able to punt the ball well with either foot. Here the sequence of shots for the left-footed punt closely monitors the previous sequence for the right-footed punt.

DROP KICK

There are two different styles of drop kick used by leading players which are both successful in their own way, but it is best to concentrate on learning one method and perfecting that. Some players, as in place kicking, prefer to kick the ball straight on.

Straight on drop kick

1. For this kick, the ball is held upright with one hand on either side.

2. The run-up is straight and the back swing of the right leg is directly back and straight forward.

3. The follow-through is also in a straight line to encourage accuracy.

Though many good drop-goal experts use this method, it is easier for beginners to use the round-the-corner method; if you are beginning from scratch, then I suggest you start with this method and stick to it. This is the more popular method at every level of the game, just as the great majority of place kickers now kick round-the-corner style.

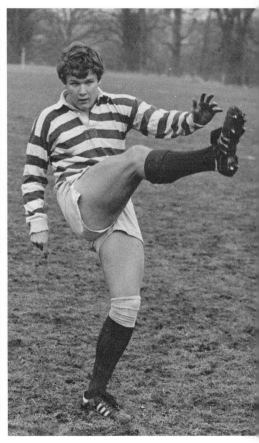

Round-the-corner drop kick

1. The ball, once again, is held upright, with one hand down each side, fingers pointing towards the ground and body side on to the post.

2. Take one step forward to place all your bodyweight on the left leg, with your head well over the ball. The ball should be dropped to land on the ground at exactly the same angle it leaves your hands and tilted slightly towards you. As the ball is dropped, your right leg begins to swing smoothly through in a full arc. At the very moment the ball touches the ground it is lifted up in the air by your right instep.

3. With your weight still on the left leg and your head remaining down, swing your right leg right through to complete the arc. A good, smooth follow-through is vital.

PLACE KICKING

Like drop kicking, there are two commonly used methods of place kicking: straight-on and round-the-corner. Again, it is really a matter of preference which you use, but for the budding goal kicker about to choose for the first time, I suggest the round-the-corner method as the more popular in Britain and the easier art to acquire.

Straight-on place kick

1. Once again, the ball is placed upright in the ground, but for this kick the six or eight paces back should be in a straight line. After a final look at the post, begin the run-up in a straight line with your head down and your eyes on the ball.

2. As before, your left foot lands just a few inches to the left of the ball and a couple of inches short of it. Your left leg supports the full weight while your right leg swings back in a straight line.

3. Your right leg swings straight through to meet the ball with the toes rather than the instep. The kicker follows through in a straight line to ensure accuracy.

Round-the-corner place kick

1. Line up the kick accurately. Make certain the hole is deep enough to ensure that the ball will not topple over. The ball should be virtually upright. Having lined up the ball and retreated six or eight paces at an angle of approximately 45 degrees, take a final look at the post.

2. The run-up should be at a steady pace and it is important to maintain the same relaxed rhythm every time you kick at goal. Your eyes should be fixed on the ball from the start of the run-up until after the ball has been kicked.

3. With your head well over the ball, your left foot lands just to the left of the ball and fractionally short of it. Your full bodyweight is now on your left leg.

4. Your right leg swings through in a smooth, full arc and follows through slightly across and in front of your body.

PRACTICE

To practise all these different kicks it is best to work in pairs. For punting, it must be stressed that players should concentrate on developing technique rather than trying to find out how far or how high they can kick a rugby ball.

Initially, they should stand about 10 or 12 metres apart and gently chip the ball to each other, concentrating on holding the ball correctly and ensuring it lands on the boot at the right angle. Gradually, over a period of weeks, the distance can be extended, provided the technique has been mastered. It is important to practise punting with both feet alternately at every training session to encourage the right technique from the beginning.

Once timing, style and accuracy are pretty good, the players can kick along a line to develop real precision kicking. One of the worst crimes any player can commit is to miss a touch kick from inside his own 22 and give the opposition a gilt-edged attacking opportunity. The two players should stand one on either side of a line – goal line, touch line, 10-metre line or

either 22 – and practise kicking across that line and using it as an imaginary touch line. The players can change over halfway through the session to give the other foot some practice. The players can start from wide angles to make it easier but, after a few weeks, if they make steady improvement the angles can gradually be tightened.

Once the players look competent, the match situation can be simulated with one or two attackers rushing at the kicker to put pressure on him. The punt as an attacking weapon can be practised by one player running at his partner, chipping it delicately over his head and running forward to try to catch it. Drop kicking and place kicking can be practised in pairs, one player standing on either side of the goal posts and kicking alternately backwards and forwards. Only the team's regular kickers should be encouraged to spend time practising these kicks.

SUMMARY

1. In punting the ball, never throw it up in the air before kicking – always release it straight down, or even push it down, so that it meets your boot at the angle at which it was originally held. Keep your foot pointed and always follow through.

2. Timing and rhythm are far more important than sheer muscle power.

3. Accuracy when punting the ball is far more important than length.

4. Your weight should be taken entirely on your left leg when kicking with your right leg and vice versa.

5. For every type of kick, keep your head well down over the ball and your eyes glued to the ball until contact has been made; exactly like golf, head down and watch the ball until you have hit it.

6. Practise under pressure once confidence has been established, because the crisis situation is when a player is being severely pressurized. A sound technique should survive intact.

6 Line-Out

No matter how talented a line-out jumper is, his ultimate success depends to a great extent on the skills of several other players. In exactly the same way as the hooker relies on a combination of the other seven forwards to lock the scrum and the scrum half to put the ball in properly, so the jumper at a line-out is utterly dependent on the person throwing in the ball and the support forwards immediately in front of and behind him to protect him. However, if the throw-in is poor, there is nothing the rest of the pack can do. I must say I was exceptionally fortunate throughout my international career and at club level to have excellent hookers to throw in.

In order to allow the blind-side wing to hang back 10 metres at the line-out to act as an extra man either in attack or defence, it is usual nowadays for the hooker to throw in. The person throwing in has four particular facets on which to concentrate all his energies. I regard accuracy as the most important, because without deadly accuracy, line-outs become a lottery. After this, in close succession, the throw should be at the right speed, the right height at the finish and the right elevation from the moment it leaves the hooker's hands until the jumper catches or palms the ball.

The timing between the thrower-in and the jumper is crucial and throughout my days as a lock forward I survived on very simple guidelines. When the hooker took the ball back behind his head prior to throwing in, I would watch him like a hawk until his hands stopped moving back in that the single steady smooth movement. The split second he stopped, I knew he would then throw it in immediately and at that moment I began my jump. I had the distinct advantage of being in front of the opposite front jumper, which meant I was already in the air before my opposite number had left the ground. I could also, by a verbal code or a prearranged signal such as a nod of the head or by holding up a certain number of fingers, ask the hooker to increase or decrease the speed of any particular throw or increase or decrease the height of the throw. This kept the opposition front jumper guessing as to what was likely to happen at every line-out on my ball and gave me the initiative.

Just as the good fly half will not always stand in exactly the same spot and run at precisely the same angle from every scrum or line-out for fear of becoming too predictable, a good jumper will vary the play at each line-out. Not only will he ask for a fast, hard, low throw at one line-out and perhaps a slow, lobbed ball at the next, he will vary his own jumping. He may jump straight up and down at the first line-out, take a short or long step forward or a short or long step backward before jumping at the next. If there is this variation in his own jumping position as well as in the speed, height and general elevation of the hooker's throw-in, the opposition will have plenty to think about during the match. None the less, in the final analysis everything depends on the thrower-in, and it is only right to start this chapter with the best technique for this highly specialized skill.

Bill Beaumont soaring above the opposition to take a two-handed catch at the front of a line-out during an England–France match

THROW-IN

1. At the outset the ball is held in both hands at the near end in front of the body, pointing directly at the line-out. A right-handed thrower will stand with his left leg forward and his weight evenly distributed on both legs.

2. With his eyes fixed on the target area, the thrower-in pulls the ball back in one hand, elbow bent, and arching his back ready to provide the momentum for the delivery. It is at the exact moment in which the thrower-in reaches this position that the jumper begins his leap in the knowledge that the ball will be thrown in immediately.

3. The hooker then rocks gently forward with his weight transferred mainly onto his left leg, straightening his back and gradually straightening his elbow as he delivers the ball in a single, continuous movement, while his arm and body follow through.

4. As he follows through, he turns his right hand over to generate the torpedo throw which gives greater accuracy and makes life easier for his line-out jumper.

No matter what particular type of throw the jumper wants on any particular occasion, the basic technique is exactly the same as demonstrated here.

JUMPING FOR THE BALL

There are many different types of line-out jump in common use nowadays and which one is the best depends on the circumstances at any given time. Often, the two-handed catch is best as it is not only the most decisive but it also stops the opposition backs advancing within 10 metres of the line-out (otherwise they would be offside). It is, needless to say, the most difficult, especially in the middle of the line or at the back. This is the most useful ball for the backs in attack because the opposition tail-end forwards are committed in the line-out.

It is easier to take a low, hard, two-handed catch at the front, but this is less useful for the backs in launching an attack. The most popular method of winning a line-out is to palm the ball to the scrum half. It is, however, worth every jumper being adept at each of the variations.

Front jump

As a front jumper, I often, but not always, tended to take a step into the jump, whilst at the same time jumping very slightly across into the ball. On my ball, I knew the signal, and after communicating with the hooker, I knew the exact destination, speed, height and trajectory of the throw. With that knowledge, which my immediate opponent did not share, I felt like a hooker on his own put-in at the set scrum – I should always win my own ball. I always took off fractionally before the opposition and there-fore I expected to arrive at the point of impact first.

The ball is thrown in fast, low and hard, and the jumper here is already in the air to meet it. He has jumped to his left, slightly across the line,

to catch the ball two-handed. Front-jumping requires great concentration, determination and quick reflexes to win and secure possession. The jumper also requires blocking by his props in front and behind him.

On the opposition throw-in to the front, I tried to anticipate the throw and I did everything in my power to get the ball first. At worst, I could make it as hard as possible for my opponent to make a two-handed catch. If I could not win a line-out ball clearly, I would challenge aggressively for the ball, usually forcing the opposition into winning, untidy, poor-quality possession.

Two-handed catch, middle of the line

The same attributes of concentration, determination, agility and timing are needed as for the front jump, but, even with a good leap and a perfect throw, a two-handed catch is not always possible. It should be remembered that with this longer throw so much more can go wrong. The ball is in the air that much longer and this gives the opposition more time to contest the throw. The best line-out expert in the side usually jumps in the middle, but he relies to a great extent on the accuracy, speed and trajectory of the throw and the support of his pack. If he is a much better jumper than the opposite team's middle jumper and the throwing-in is spot on, he may well win the line-out with a succession of two-handed catches, but if there is little to choose between himself and his opponent, he may well have to resort to palming the ball. As we have mentioned before, variations can help a middle jumper. The ball can be lobbed higher occasionally, thrown in a little faster or a shade slower, and the jumper can take half a step forward or backwards on a given signal from the jumper to the thrower-in to catch the opposition off guard.

Palming

Palming the ball is the easiest way to win possession in the middle or at the back of the line, but it can also be the most dangerous if it is not done with great care and consideration. The ball should never be slapped willy-nilly out of the line-out, but should be carefully guided with one hand or with two hands towards the scrum half.

1. Here, the jumper has ascertained where the scrum half is standing before the ball is thrown in. With that fact uppermost in his mind, he has jumped up with his eyes riveted on the ball until he has won possession. The moment he has won the ball, he looks immediately for his scrum half to guide it safely into his hands.

2. Similarly, the jumper can ensure even greater control and accuracy if he uses two hands, though he will not be able to jump quite as high as he can when palming with one hand.

SUPPORT PLAY

Once the thrower-in and the jumper are working in perfect harmony and the ball has been won, there is still plenty to be done by the rest of the pack in support to secure good possession. Whether the ball is won at the front, middle or back, the jumper relies heavily on solid support and protection. In a seven-man line-out, when the jumper has won the ball, the other six forwards have to contribute in varying degrees to make certain that good-quality ball reaches the scrum half. It is a combined effort on the part of all the forwards.

Blocking in support

1. The low, hard throw to the front is about to be taken at head height in this illustration and the jumper has, in midair, turned his back on the opposition as he is about to win possession, to protect the ball.

2. At the same instance as he catches it, his two props have bound tightly onto him to make the ball totally secure from stray opposition hands or bodies.

3. The rest of the pack have now joined the drive and are equally distributed on either side of the jumper to give him complete stability and security.

Middle jump

Similarly, with a two-handed catch in the middle, the jumper will be engulfed by support the moment he takes the ball. In this illustration, the three players standing in front of him in the line have all turned to face the opposition and are bound firmly on to him to protect him fully from any interference. The player immediately behind the jumper has rushed in to shore up any gap through which the opposition might encroach, and the two back markers in the line are making swift tracks to lend their support.

Back of the line

In an evenly contested line-out, the long throw to the back will invariably be palmed back either to the scrum half for a quick attacking ball or to a large forward for a peel round the back of the line-out to launch himself against the opposition midfield back. The first option involves quick possession to the backs with the opposition loose forwards tied in; this is just about the best quality of ball from which to attack. The second can give the backs superb second-phase ball if the forwards do their work well.

THE PEEL

As these illustrations show, the ball is thrown to end of the line-out to the penultimate player. He usually is the tallest member of the back row or at least the best jumper (normally the number 8) but quite often, as a surprise tactic, teams switch their best jumper to that position from the front or the middle of the line-out just for the peel move.

1. This player jumps high and, two-handed, palms the ball out of the line-out, guiding it not out towards the threequarter line or even straight out of the line-out at 90 degrees, but fractionally back towards the touch line. This is in the direction and path of the prop, who was originally standing at number 3 in the line-out.

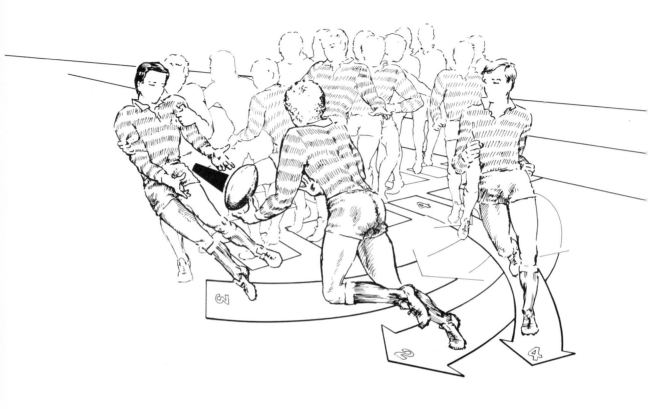

2. He takes the ball on the burst close to the set piece and, rounding the end of the line-out, drives straight into the opposition loose forwards at the tail of the line-out.

3. As he commits them totally and is tackled, he feeds a short pass to his nearest support player on the outside, probably the front-jumping lock forward who would have been standing originally at number 2 in the seven-man line. He should set off towards the opposition midfield trio to cause as much havoc and consternation as possible with the support of the other lock forward on his outside. This is how I organized the peel during my career with Fylde, England and the Lions. However, a side could use different players, depending on the various strengths and weaknesses in key positions. If, for example, one of the locks or the props is an especially bad handler, then another player should be used instead.

The forwards should be able to win quick loose ball, at worst, from this situation, which the backs should be able to use to good advantage.

The illustration also shows the angles and the concept of the peel, which can be devastatingly effective if done well.

SHORTENED LINE-OUTS

If a team is finding itself hopelessly outjumped on its own throw-in at every point in the line-out, then the best solution is to try shortened line-outs. Smaller, lighter sides, like the Japanese, have wrought miracles in recent years by changing the emphasis of a line-out. They no longer make it a straight test of jumping ability between the respective lock forwards on each side, but more of a test of agility, speed of thought and quick-witted reflexes and reactions – a subtle blend of the unexpected, unusual and occasionally outrageous.

Two-man line-outs are useful ploys not only for sides having difficulty winning full line-outs for any reason, but also as a variation to disrupt the opposition's standard defensive organization. The main advantage of a short line-out is that it gives the initiative very firmly to the side throwing in. That side dictates exactly what will happen, when and how, and because there are only two players from each side in the line-out, it is much harder for the opposition to disrupt a jumper illegally. The referee can see more easily exactly what is going on.

The skills required to win a short line-out are slightly different from the pure jumping at full line-out. It is because of this that a small, agile, mobile lock has been known comprehensively to outjump a 6-foot 6-inch giant of a lock. A two-man line-out is no longer a straight up and down contest on the spot. It is more a question of out-manoeuvring one's opponent to leave oneself jumping virtually alone for the ball.

There are many different ways of achieving this objective and overleaf we demonstrate the two most common which have been hugely successful in recent years. The best exponent during my playing career was Jean-Luc Joinel of France, who combined superb timing, manoeuvrability, lightning reflexes and a perfect understanding with both the thrower-in and his

Bill Beaumont reaches great heights in the line-out – England against Wales 1979-80

scrum half constantly to outwit the opposition and win countless two-man line-outs at international level. The secret of a successful two-man line is the ability to move forward and backward rapidly into space with a permanent split-second advantage over the opposition. You know exactly where and when and at what trajectory the ball will come.

1. In this sequence the two players stand about two metres apart ready for the ball to be thrown in.

2. As the thrower-in takes the ball back behind his head, the second man in the line-out runs quickly backward two or three paces. His opponent, caught unawares, immediately springs backward to mark him.

3. As the thrower-in releases the ball, his jumper, having abruptly stopped moving backward, moves quickly forward into the gap, leaving his opponent trying desperately to switch from sprinting backward to sprinting forward in the same moment to counter him.

It is inevitable that the player calling all the shots and in full knowledge of exactly what is meant to happen will win the line-out. Hence an agile 5-foot forward can outwit a 6-foot jumper to win the ball.

In the same way, the jumper can execute exactly the opposite manoeuvre in the same situation.

1. The jumper stands as in the first sequence, ready for the ball to be thrown in. As the thrower-in takes the ball back behind his head, the jumper, having first leaned back on the spot to encourage his opponent to consider doing likewise, immediately leans sharply forward to persuade his opponent he is about to jump forward and up into the gap.

2. With the opposition jumper's full momentum now driving him forward, our jumper is ready to drive backward off his left leg to leave his opponent stranded.

3. Unmarked, he is able to win the ball comfortably. Similar ploys can be used with a three-man line-out in which either the second or third jumper can outwit his opponent, adding more permutations and confusion further to outfox the opposition.

All this goes to prove the line-out is not simply a question of two people jumping as high as possible in the air at any given time. It is much more complex than that and good line-out play is the end product of hours and hours of practice. It is partly the result of individual skills, but it is much more than that. It requires a concerted effort from the whole pack.

PRACTICE

During my career I found that squat jumps were the best exercise for improving my line-out jumping. I used to do a sequence of about twenty squats, take a short rest, and then do another twenty, trying to touch the same spot as high up a goal post or a lamppost or a wall as possible on each of the forty leaps.

The other exercise which I did regularly was to leap as high as possible and clap my hands in the air. To measure improvement, this can be done using a clothesline as a guide. Raise the level at which you can clap your hands above the clothesline as you gradually improve your jumping. Again, a burst of twenty squats in succession builds up stamina.

Individual practice with someone to throw in is the next stage, and when a good basic technique has been established, this can be improved in pressure situations.

After you have gained confidence jumping alone with just the hooker throwing in, it is excellent practice to use a second competent thrower-in and two scrum halfs as well. The first thrower-in should stand in the normal place on the touch line, the second thrower-in op-posite him on the 15-metre dotted line in the field of play, with the jumper in the middle and one scrum half on each side of the jumper. The jumper faces the hooker on the touch line who throws the ball in. The jumper catches it, immediately feeds the scrum half and instantly turns right round to face the second thrower-in. He throws the ball in at once and the jumper catches it, feeds the other scrum half straight-away, then turns round to face the hooker on the touch line again. Meanwhile the hooker has received the original ball back from the first scrum half and is ready to throw in again. The process is repeated so the jumper receives ten throws from each thrower-in without a break. After twenty line-outs he can have a three-mi-nute rest. At each session he should undertake three sequences of twenty throws with two short rest periods as he improves; it is also possible to introduce opposition. Initially one player can jump against him, and this can be increased to two and even three players. When a satisfactory standard has been achieved, sup-port players can be added to produce the per-fect end product.

SUMMARY

1. Timing of the jump is crucial. It is essential to know on each throw where, when and at what elevation the ball is being thrown to time the jump accordingly.
2. Try to catch the ball cleanly with two hands if possible, but, if not, guide it accurately back to the scrum half with a one- or two-handed palm. Do not slap it wildly anywhere just for the sake of winning the line-out.
3. Insist on good, accurate throwing and quick, solid support from the rest of the pack.

4. When jumping into the ball, turn your back slightly towards the opposition to ensure the ball is protected from any stray hands.
5. Bend the knees as you prepare to jump to enable you to drive upwards with maximum impetus.
6. Keep your eyes on the ball all the time.
7. If you cannot outjump your opponent, then try to outwit and outmanoeuvre him. Quick reactions and agility can win line-out ball.

Bill Beaumont takes a two-handed catch at the front of a line-out against Ireland at Twickenham in 1978

7 Set Scrummage

Scrummaging is one of the most demanding aspects of the game but it is also one of the most satisfying. The most important thing to remember is that, more than any other part of the game, scrummaging is a team effort by the whole pack – all eight forwards have to work together and, if one individual decides to take a breather, it adversely affects the whole unit.

The key figure is the hooker. He is the one who strikes to win the ball, but his ultimate success is entirely dependent on the efforts of the other seven forwards and, of course, the scrum half, who must put the ball into the scrum consistently at the same speed and to the same spot every time. The scrum half should only feed the scrum when it is steady and stable, not when it is being pushed back or wheeled askew.

The ideal scrum should be very tightly bound. The forwards should pack and scrummage with their full bodyweight to exert the maximum pressure on the opposing scrum. As a lock forward, it was my job to lock the scrum to give our hooker the chance to win the ball and guide it back.

The England pack, solid and stable on their own put-in, work together to win clean possession against Scotland

HOOKER

In exactly the same way as a line-out jumper relies on a good throw-in and the support of the rest of the pack to protect him, so the hooker relies on a scrum half to concentrate on a consistent feed at the right time and on the rest of the pack to absorb the full pressure of the opposition.

The scrum half and the hooker should practise the put-in at a goal post or with both props on a scrummaging machine until they are satisfied precisely how the hooker wants the ball delivered.

1. In this illustration the hooker is in the position he would adopt in a scrum: his right foot is slightly forward and his weight primarily on his left leg. In a good scrummaging position, the hooker's backside will be just below the level of his shoulders to enable him to withstand the pressure exerted on the front row by the opposing team. From this stance, he also has enough room to shoot his right foot forward the moment the ball is fed into the scrum. His right shoulder should be dropped slightly to restrict the opposition hooker's view of the ball.

2. As the ball is put in, the hooker, with his right foot, strikes diagonally forward towards the opposition tight-head prop to meet the ball as it lands inside the tunnel. Initially, at schoolboy level, the signal for the hooker to strike is usually given by the scrum half, who says

something like 'Now' as he puts the ball in. On the command 'Now', the hooker strikes at the spot where he expects the ball to land, usually on the ground directly under his own loose-head prop's right shoulder.

When players become more sophisticated they can progress to 'flapping'. This means that the hooker gives the signal to the scrum half rather than the other way round. Normally, this is not a verbal signal; instead the hooker raises his left hand, which is binding just beside the scrum half's head as he crouches down with the ball. The moment the scrum half sees the hand 'flap', he feeds the ball into the scrum. His hooker is ready but the opposition hooker is not as he has not seen or heard any signal.

Whichever method is used, the put-in must be at the same speed and to the same place every time. This consistency is vital for the hooker. As the ball lands, the hooker strikes with the inside of his right foot and then sweeps the ball back in one continuous movement. This follow-through is very important. Once he has guided the ball back, he should resume a scrummaging position to help keep the scrum stable or even drive the opposition back. At every scrum, the hooker requires 100 per cent concentration, with his eyes riveted to the ball, and quick reactions to adjust instantly to a poor put-in or a twisting or retreating scrum.

FRONT ROW

A tight, solid front row is essential to a good scrum and that means the binding must be firm with bodies and feet at the right angles and in the right positions.

1. The hooker is the central figure and he should stand ready to go down with his hands and arms free to bind onto his props.

2. The hooker binds over the shoulders of his props and his hands grip tightly on their shirts just under their outside arms. The props each grip the hooker equally firmly around the waist.

3. From the back, the binding and the positioning of the props are clear. The tight-head prop (3) should keep his left shoulder and hip right beside his hooker to push him towards the ball; there should be no gap between them. For scrummaging this prop will have both feet back and fractionally less than a shoulder-width apart. The loose-head prop will pack flush against his hooker with his feet more than a shoulder-width apart and his right leg just behind his hooker's left leg. Gripping firmly, they are now ready to pack down as a tightly knit, secure unit.

LOCKS

1. The two locks bind tightly together, gripping each other's shorts at waist level.

2. When the scrum prepares to pack down, they should each go down on the inside knee ready to take one step forward as they drive into the scrum. This means they do not need to move their feet back at all and the scrum is solidly locked. The locks should have straight backs and their heads should be held up, looking straight ahead.

3. If the front row is bound as tightly as it should be, the two locks should have to work very hard to force their heads through. They then firmly grip the shorts of the respective props at waist level with their outside arms.

4. This shows the locks bound together after they have forced their heads between the hooker and the respective props and just before they drive forwards and upwards into the scrum.

5. Once the scrum is steady, the locks will achieve the greatest purchasing power by splaying their feet at a comfortable distance about a shoulder-width apart. With their boots

at this angle, the majority of the studs are in direct contact with the ground to give them maximum leverage.

6. This illustrates the feet position of the loose-head prop and the left lock and also their straight backs. From this stance they can absorb the weight and drive from the opposition and at the same time efficiently transmit their own forward power and momentum.

LOOSE FORWARDS

1. At the same time as the front five scrum down, the flank forwards bind firmly at a slight angle onto the respective props, gripping the shorts of the second row, with their inside shoulders pushing against the top of the thigh of each prop's outside leg.

2. The shove and drive of the two flankers is of enormous help to the two props and, in consequence, to the general solidity of the whole scrummage. Each flanker should scrum with a flat back, head held up and both feet back; the outside foot should be just in front of the inside foot.

3. The number 8 joins the scrum by forcing his head between the two locks, his shoulders pushing on their buttocks and his arms binding round their legs, holding firmly onto their shorts.

4. In these examples we have illustrated how each position should go down in a set scrum, but, it must be stressed, ideally all eight forwards should go down together at exactly the same time to give maximum solidity to the scrum.

CHANELLED HEEL

There are three basic channels through which to heel the ball at a scrum and the diagrams show them clearly.

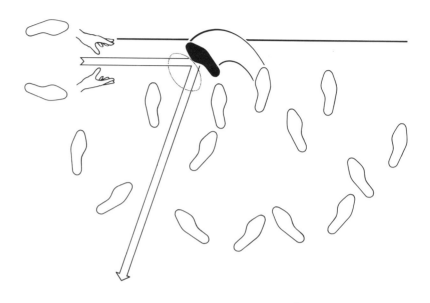

Channel one

For channel-one ball, the hooker strikes and sweeps the ball straight out between the legs of his loose-head prop and through the gap between the flanker, who packs at an angle, and the left lock. No sooner is the ball fed into the scrum than it reappears in play almost at once. The scrum half must be very alert because his opposite number will be right on top of him if he fails to scoop the ball up and deliver his pass in one rapid movement. This is the fastest heel of all, but because the scrum half has minimal protection, it is also the one most fraught with risk. It is usually done when your pack is under severe pressure in the scrum and is either being marched back on the retreat or wheeled and disrupted to give the halfbacks poor-quality possession. It can also be done on the attack when the backs want really quick ball from the scrum.

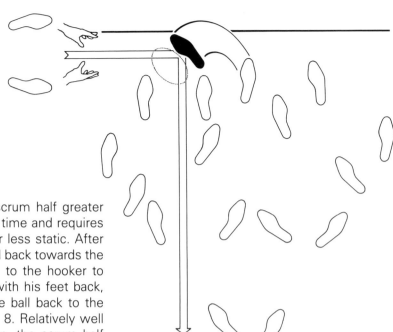

Channel two

Channel-two ball gives the scrum half greater protection, but it takes more time and requires the scrum to remain more or less static. After the hooker has swept the ball back towards the feet of the left lock, it is up to the hooker to resume scrummaging hard with his feet back, while the lock negotiates the ball back to the left-hand side of the number 8. Relatively well protected from the oppositon, the scrum half has a little more time to send out an accurate pass to his fly half.

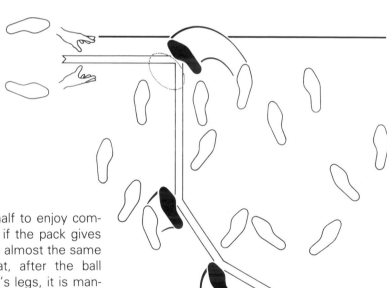

Channel three

It is possible for the scrum half to enjoy complete security and protection if the pack gives him channel-three ball. This is almost the same as channel two, except that, after the ball passes between the left lock's legs, it is man-oeuvred across from the left- to the right-hand side of the number 8. Channel-three ball is the safest type of possession in defence and gives your team the greatest control. It is also from this possession that most back-row moves originate.

BACK-ROW MOVES

It can become too predictable and too easy to defend against if a team invariably spins the ball along the threequarter line from every scrum. For this reason, it is extremely useful to unleash the occasional back-row move. This is designed to draw the opposition loose forwards and give the backs less cover defence to negotiate when they get the ball from the ruck or maul which will inevitably ensue. Secondly, it should make the opposition check their defensive duties round the periphery of the scrum for the rest of the game. Instead of sprinting across the field trying to disrupt your backs, they must wait until the scrum half has passed out in case a back-row move is attempted. There is a variety of back-row moves and here are examples of a couple of the best.

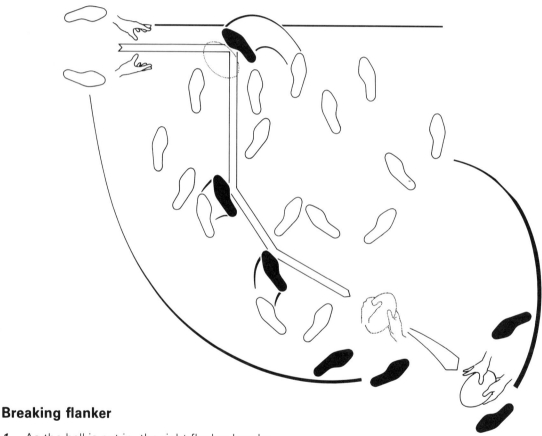

Breaking flanker

1. As the ball is put in, the right flanker breaks away and immediately retreats behind the scrum. After securing quick, good channel-three possession, the scrum half flicks a short pass to the flanker, who drives round behind the scrum and into the opposing flank forward and, perhaps, the number 8.

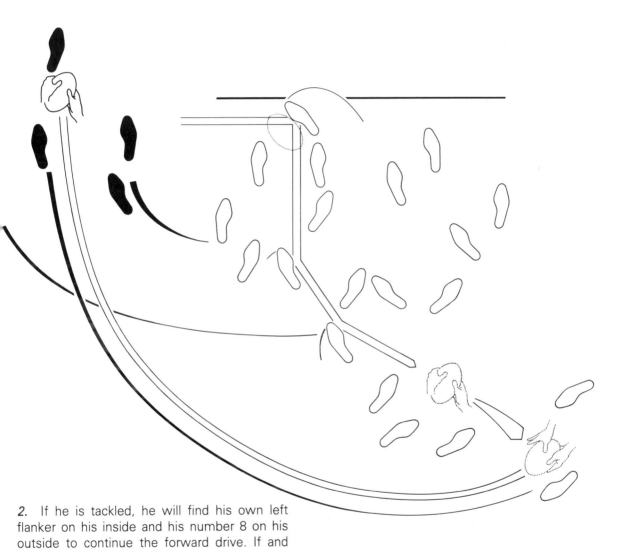

2. If he is tackled, he will find his own left flanker on his inside and his number 8 on his outside to continue the forward drive. If and when the move is halted, all three opposing loose forwards will have been absorbed into the ensuing ruck or maul to leave your back division in a commanding position to attack with the loose ball.

Breaking scrum half

1. This requires good channel-three possession and a stable platform. The scrum half
gives a signal to the number 8 (verbally or with
a slap on the leg) and he sprints rapidly a few
yards to his right.

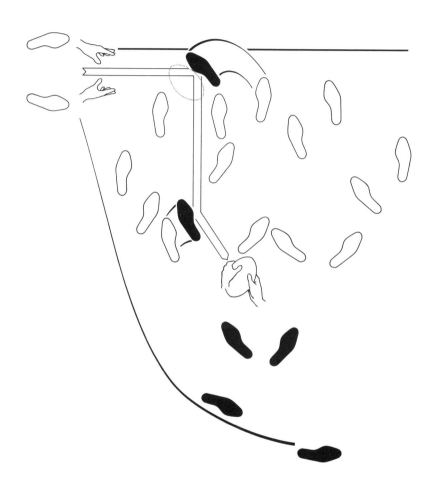

2. As he sets off, the number 8 picks up the ball and, with his back to the opposing scrum half, feeds a short, flat pass to his own scrum half. The gain line is quickly crossed, and the right flanker and the number 8 should sweep through in support, one on either side of the scrum half.

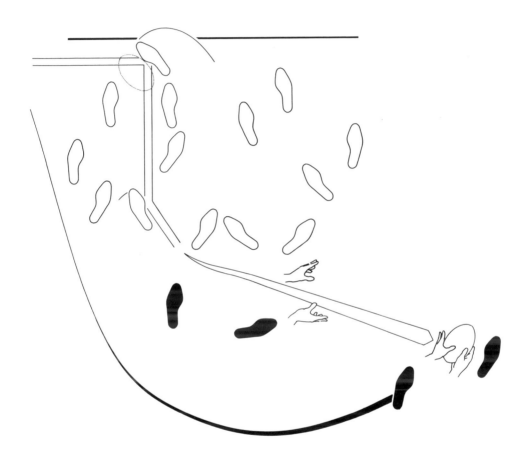

PRACTICE

The first exercise for young players learning how to scrummage is to work in pairs and push against each other. Great care should be taken to match individuals of similar size, bulk and strength to minimize the risk of injury. This is of paramount importance, particularly in the case of very young players. Youngsters will rapidly learn the problems and the pitfalls of scrummaging and the benefits of a sound technique.

For one-to-one scrummaging, feet should be about a shoulder-width apart and knees bent, ready to impart the full body momentum. Backs should be arched to transmit the full thrust from the legs through to the shoulders, which should be driving forward and upward. The head should be up all the time.

Maintaining all these principles, the next stage should be in groups of four. Here two players push against another two, binding tightly on to each other. When this has been done satisfactorily, a full front-row situation can be attempted with three pushing against three.

Still keeping the groups evenly matched, a pair of locks can be added to each side to allow five players to scrummage against another five. Eventually they can be joined by a number 8. Finally, the flankers can be added and the pushing contest continued. At this stage a ball can be introduced, although it need not be used all the time. This sequence of events can be built up over several training sessions.

Players get the feel of a scrum much better if they are pushing against live opposition, but if the two packs are not well matched, it can do more harm than good. When one pack is bigger, heavier and stronger than the other, it subjects the opposition to unfair and intolerable pressure. There is also a risk of injury. If the packs are evenly matched, they can have little contests, going for pushover tries from scrum fives and taking it in turns to defend. If they are badly matched, it may be safer to practise with a scrummaging machine.

Although live scrummaging is the ideal form of practice, great benefit can be gained from using a scrummaging machine. It is well worth practising the eight-man shove on your opponent's ball against a machine. The eight forwards dip their bodies, straighten their legs and drive forward and upward in unison on the command of the pack leader as the ball is fed into the scrum. The techniques for the various channelled heels and all back-row moves can also be practised using a scrummaging machine.

When the various techniques have been perfected using a machine, they should be practised against a live pack of similar size and strength if at all possible. Regular bursts of intensive, concentrated scrummaging practice should be organized at every training session. A really good scrum lays the foundations of a really good team.

SUMMARY

1. Every player must be tightly bound for a solid, effective scrum.

2. Each player must be in the best position to help transmit the drive from behind and to absorb the pressure from the oppositon.

3. Every player should pack low, with a straight back and bent knees, feet a comfortable distance apart, shoulders in a position to transmit the drive forward and upward, the head well up, and poised ready to straighten as the ball comes in.

4. The scrum should be a tightly knit unit with everyone firmly gripping his colleagues. The players should all squeeze together in perfect harmony to drive forward as the ball is put into the scrum. Ideally the scrum should go forward; in reality a team does well to hold steady. Either way, it must be a unified drive if it is to be fully effective.

5. The efficiency of whichever channelled heel is called at any particular scrum remains a collective effort on the part of all eight forwards.

6. Occasional back-row moves add variety and unpredictability, posing problems for the opposition.

7. On the opposition put-in, make life as difficult as possible: try the eight-man shove to push them right off the ball or wheel them round in an arc to destroy the quality of their possession.

8 Ruck and Maul

Nowadays more tries are scored from loose ball than from possession won directly at the set pieces, although it is still extremely useful to dominate the scrums and line-outs because that inevitably makes it much easier to control the rucks and the mauls.

Most teams are so well organized in defence that it is very hard to score by simply passing the ball along the three-quarter line even if an extra man joins the line and manages to create an overlap. More often than not the cover defence will have swept across the pitch to thwart the initial threat, but if the attacking side can then win quick second-phase possession, a score may well materialize.

In this case, the opposing loose forwards will be temporarily out of action at the bottom of a ruck or wrestling in the middle of a maul; breaching the defence then becomes much simpler. None the less, it is important to win first-phase ball – scrums and line-outs – as, once in possession, it is much more likely your team will win the second-phase – rucks or mauls – when the initial move eventually breaks down. The higher the standard of play, the more likely it is that set-piece possession will not be an end in itself, but a means to an end.

It should be emphasized that the team in possession of the ball who set up the ruck or the maul have no divine right to expect automatically to win the ensuing ruck or maul. The odds are stacked in their favour, but they must have a sound technique and follow a few important rules.

The player carrying the ball at the time the initial attack is on the point of breaking down must ensure that every effort is taken to make the ball available to his supporting players the instant he is checked. It naturally follows that his support players must make certain they arrive as quickly as possible at the point of the breakdown – at very worst, a fraction of a second before the opposition. It must be a collective commitment from the whole pack involving all eight forwards and any back who happens to be in the immediate vicinity.

The basic difference between a ruck and a maul is that in a ruck the ball is on the ground and in a maul it is off the ground in a player's hands.

Paul Lavin of Lancashire feeds his scrum half Steve Smith during a Roses match against Yorkshire

A tightly bound maul results in maximum protection for England scrum half Nick Youngs as Nick Jeavons releases the ball for England against Ireland

RUCK

1. The player with the ball drives forward into the opposition and hits the defenders with his full body momentum as he is tackled. At that precise moment he dips his shoulder into the two tacklers to knock them backwards and to force his body between the opposition and the ball.

2. As the attacker falls in the tackle, he instantly releases the ball by placing it on the ground on his own team's side of his body just before he completes his fall.

3. At the same moment as he lands on the ground and loses all contact with the ball after the tackle, it is crucial for the first two support players to arrive to protect and secure the ball. They should arrive together, binding firmly onto each other as they drive, low and hard, into the opposition.

4. A split second later, the bulk of the pack should arrive and, binding tightly onto each other, drive aggressively into the ruck from at least 3, and preferably 5, metres away, with their backs straight and, ideally, parallel to the ground. They should keep their eyes glued on the ball all the time and, virtually ignoring it, they should drive over the ball and any bodies on the ground to leave the ball stationary for the scrum half to feed to his backs.

5. Making sure if possible that every player remains on his feet throughout the manoeuvre, and watching the ball all the time to avoid kicking it through to the opposition, the forwards continue to drive over the tackled player, leaving the ball exactly where it was originally placed ready for the scrum half. If the ruck appears to be stuck, each player should start pumping flat out with his feet in the hope of driving forward. If every forward does this, the united effort should edge the ruck forward to win the ball. At worst, the referee should award the subsequent scrum to the team going forward.

6. The last members of the pack to arrive link together and drive into the ruck, low and hard, stepping over the ball and any tackled players on the ground. As a last resort, if they are completely checked and held, they can attempt to heel the ball.

Good rucking depends on sound technique, tremendous speed and firm binding.

MAUL

Just as in the ruck, it is vital in the maul for the first three support players to arrive as quickly as possible. The moment the player carrying the ball meets the opposition, he is in a vulnerable position and, to ensure winning the maul, he must have instant support. Again, the whole pack must drive into the maul low and hard, with straight backs and heads up, not just as they thunder into the maul but from a full 5 metres away.

1. As with the ruck, the ball-carrier dips his shoulder and turns his back to the defender at the moment he takes the tackle. To remain upright, it is important to spread the feet wide apart to give a solid base.

2. In the maul, the tackled player must stay on his feet and, by holding the ball at arm's length in outstretched hands, he secures and protects the ball from the opposition as the first support player arrives, ideally, simultaneously.

3. The first player to arrive immediately takes the ball from the tackled player and, at the same time, turns his back to the opposition further to protect the ball. He also adopts a wide stance with his feet, with knees bent, and holds the ball low in outstretched hands.

4. With the original ball-carrier acting as a buffer, it is vital the next two support players arrive almost at once, one on either side, to form an impenetrable wedge to guarantee retaining possession. These two players should explode into the maul to drive it forward. They should prepare to hit the maul hard, with their bodies low to the ground, backs straight and heads up. This posture must be adopted not at the moment of entry but from 5 metres away.

5. Similarly, from at least 5 metres distance, the rest of the pack should thunder into the maul low and hard, equally distributed with two players on the left of the ball and two players on the right.

In illustrating both the ruck and the maul, just as in the chapter on scrummaging, I have described the role of each player step by step in gradual progression. In reality, it must be stressed that the build-up to a ruck or a maul takes place in a hectic flurry of activity and the last players to arrive should explode into the ruck or the maul only a few seconds after it has been set up.

PRACTICE

At the outset it is a good idea to use tackling bags to practise rucking and mauling in the same way as working on a scrummaging machine to get to grips with the basic techniques of scrummaging. To practise rucking, the player with the ball drives into the tackling bags and, as he drops down in the imaginary tackle, he places the ball on the ground just behind him. The next couple of players, thundering into the ruck from about 5 metres, drive over the ball and the tackled player. The rest of the forwards follow suit, each player trying to stay on his feet as he drives over the ball.

Similarly, the maul can be practised with the ball-carrier staying on his feet as he hits the tackling bags, the first support player securing the ball and the next two players driving in on either side to offer further protection. When confidence has been developed, limited opposition can be introduced – initially perhaps a couple of defenders to halt the ball-carrier.

As the standard of loose play improves, the opposition numbers can be gradually increased until they are at full strength.

Another useful practice routine is for three players to bind together like a front row, standing with their backs to the attacking side. The five attackers run towards them, the ball-carrier drives into them while his support players ensure the ruck or the maul is won, and the scrum half collects the ball. Alternatively, the ball can be placed on the ground behind or in front of the three bound players and the five attackers can drive in to win possession.

As these skills are developed, it is possible to have three sets of three players bound together as front rows spread over a distance of 50 metres. The first group could be 15 metres in from the touch line on the 22-metre line, the next group in midfield on the 10-metre line and the third group near the touch line on the far 10-metre line. The five forwards should spring to the first group, drive them off the ball, spring to the next group and do the same thing, and then onto the third group.

From this passive opposition of three players, two full packs can be used once the players have mastered the correct techniques. The packs should be a few metres apart and the ball thrown alternately to each of them. They should then set up either a ruck or a maul against the other pack.

SUMMARY

1. The first player must keep control of the ball as he drives into the oppositon.

2. The first two or three support players must arrive almost immediately to secure and protect the ball.

3. The rest of the pack must arrive as fast as possible.

4. Players should explode into the ruck or maul from 5 metres away, low to the ground, with straight backs and heads up.

5. If at all possible, players should try to stay on their feet.

6. Try to win the ball in a ruck or a maul with your pack going forward and the opposition going backwards.

7. At rucks, do not initially try to heel the ball, but drive over it, binding tightly onto your colleagues.

8. Drive into rucks and mauls parallel to the touch line, charging directly towards the opposition goal line.